the Landing™ JOURNAL

THE LANDING™
A CELEBRATE RECOVERY® RESOURCE
STUDENT JOURNAL
Copyright © 2010 Group Publishing, Inc.

group.com
simplyyouthministry.com

Credits
Authors: John Baker, Johnny Baker, with Rick Lawrence
Executive Developer: Nadim Najm
Chief Creative Officer: Joani Schultz
Editor: Cheryl Baker
Copy Editor: Rob Cunningham
Cover Art and Production: Veronica Lucas
Production Manager: DeAnne Lear

ISBN 978-0-7644-6449-2

10 9 8 7 6 5 4   18 17 16 15 14 13 12

WELCOME TO

theLanding™

Thanks for joining us on this exciting journey here at The Landing. Each week, we'll gather together to develop deeper friendships, share ideas, watch videos, explore incredible truths from the Bible, and challenge one another through hands-on activities. And most important of all, we'll learn about God's amazing love for us.

Instead of a lecture or fill-in-the-blank style of teaching, we use music, film, high-octane discussions, and creative experiences to get at the core truths we're exploring. Along the way, we'll discover real-life strategies for making wise choices, building healthy friendships, and developing successful patterns for life. And we'll find ways to move our focus on Jesus from the fringes of everyday life to the bull's-eye of everyday life.

This journal is for YOU! Use it each week to record your thoughts and feelings. This journal is for your eyes only, so make sure to keep this in a safe place.

We look forward to being with you on this journey—learning, growing, and experiencing life together. This promises to be a life-changing adventure!

TABLE OF CONTENTS

Small Group Guidelines   1

Serenity Prayer   3

lesson 1 **DENIAL**   5

lesson 2 **DENIAL**   9

lesson 3 **POWERLESS**   13

lesson 4 **POWERLESS**   17

lesson 5 **HOPE**   23

lesson 6 **HOPE**   27

lesson 7 **PEACE**   31

lesson 8 **PEACE**   35

lesson 9 **TURN**   39

lesson 10 **TURN**   43

lesson 11 **ACTION**   47

lesson 12 **ACTION**   53

lesson 13 **HONESTY**   57

lesson 14 **HONESTY**   61

lesson 15 **COMMUNITY**   65

lesson 16 **COMMUNITY**   69

lesson 17 **INVENTORY**   75

lesson 18 **INVENTORY**   81

lesson 19 **SPIRITUAL INVENTORY**   85

lesson 20 **SPIRITUAL INVENTORY**   89

lesson 21 **SPIRITUAL INVENTORY**   93

lesson 22 **CELEBRATION**   97

lesson 23 **PRAYER STATIONS**   99

lesson 24 **CONFESS**   103

lesson 25 **CONFESS**   107

lesson 26 **ADMIT**   111

lesson 27 **ADMIT**   115

lesson 28 **READY**   119

lesson 29 **READY**   123

lesson 30 **VICTORY**   127

lesson 31 **VICTORY**   131

lesson 32 **AMENDS**   135

lesson 33 **AMENDS**   139

lesson 34 **FORGIVENESS**   143

lesson 35 **FORGIVENESS**   147

lesson 36 **CELEBRATION**   151

lesson 37 **GRACE**   153

lesson 38 **GRACE**   157

lesson 39 **PRAYER STATIONS**   161

lesson 40 **CROSSROADS**   165

lesson 41 **CROSSROADS**   169

lesson 42 **DAILY INVENTORY**   173

lesson 43 **DAILY INVENTORY**   177

lesson 44 **RELAPSE**   181

lesson 45 **RELAPSE**   187

lesson 46 **GRATITUDE**   191

lesson 47 **GRATITUDE**   195

lesson 48 **GIVE**   201

lesson 49 **GIVE**   205

lesson 50 **YES**   209

lesson 51 **YES**   213

lesson 52 **CELEBRATION**   217

SMALL GROUP GUIDELINES

1. FOCUS ON YOUR OWN THOUGHTS AND FEELINGS WHEN SHARING WITH THE GROUP.

We want to be sure everyone has time to share, so please limit your sharing to three to five minutes. If you focus on your own thoughts and feelings, you're less likely to "wander" and discuss unrelated topics. As the group leader, I may let you know when you've shared for too long, but if you focus on what matters most, you'll likely stay within the time boundaries.

2. PLEASE AVOID ALL CROSS TALK.

We want each person to be free to express feelings and thoughts without interruptions. Here are some examples of "cross talk." Two individuals engage in conversation while excluding everyone else. A group member interrupts or inappropriately laughs when another person shares. Or a group member says, "I can relate to you because..." or "I can't relate to you because...." Please be respectful toward the other members of our group, because I know you want everyone to be respectful when it's your turn to share.

3. WE ARE HERE TO SUPPORT ONE ANOTHER.

Sometimes in our group settings, we hear about other people's challenges, and we want to offer solutions to fix their problems. We may have the right intention, and we may want to share the wisdom we're gaining from being in this awesome program. But the other person may not be ready or want to hear or understand. You will protect each other by simply supporting one another and not trying to "fix" one another.

4. VALUE AND PROTECT ANONYMITY AND CONFIDENTIALITY.

It hurts to discover that information someone has shared here is being discussed outside of the small group time. Some of us struggle with trust issues because we've been hurt by other people. We all need to know that this is a safe place to share. What is shared in our group stays in our group. The only exception is if someone threatens to injure himself/herself or others.

5. AVOID OFFENSIVE LANGUAGE; IT HAS NO PLACE IN A CHRIST-CENTERED GROUP.

I'd encourage everyone in this group to follow this biblical thought, found in Ephesians 4:29—*Don't use foul or abusive language. Let everything you say be good and helpful, so that your words will be an encouragement to those who hear them.*

SERENITY PRAYER

Each week we are going to end our time together with a prayer called, The Serenity Prayer. It's short, but it sums up a lot of what we're doing here. Serenity is another word for peace. As we pray through these words, really think about what they mean. Try not to just read them or recite them, but think about what you're saying to God. Imagine talking to your friend, your Father and asking him for peace, courage, and acceptance.

God, grant me the serenity
to accept the things I cannot change,
the courage to change the things I can,
and the wisdom to know the difference.
Living one day at a time,
enjoying one moment at a time;
Accepting hardship as a pathway to peace;
Taking, as Jesus did,
this sinful world as it is;
Not as I would have it;
Trusting that you will make all things right
If I surrender to your will; So that I
may be reasonably happy in this life
and supremely happy with you forever
in the next. AMEN.

- Reinhold Niebuhr

the**Landing**

DENIAL
lesson one

PRINCIPLE 1:
Realize that I'm not God. I admit that I am powerless to control my tendency to do the wrong thing and that my life is unmanageable.

SCRIPTURAL TRUTHS:
"Happy are those who know they are spiritually poor"
(Matthew 5:3 GNT).

"I know that nothing good lives in me, that is, in my sinful nature. For I have the desire to do what is good, but I cannot carry it out" (Romans 7:18 NIV).

DENIAL lesson one

It's an exciting journey toward freedom that you're beginning to travel—but perhaps you're worried or afraid.

You may feel trapped by the past—your hurts, your guilt, your patterns of bad decisions. You can find hope and encouragement in these words: *"My friends, I don't feel that I have already arrived. But I forget what is behind, and I struggle for what is ahead" (Philippians 3:13 CEV).* None of us have arrived. We're all works in progress.

Or maybe instead of feeling trapped by the past, you're afraid of the future. You don't know if you have the strength or commitment or discipline to make this journey. You're worried about the twists, curves, and obstacles in the road ahead. You aren't sure if you're ready to change. Hebrews 13:6 (CEV) tells us: *"That should make you feel like saying, 'The Lord helps me! Why should I be afraid of what people can do to me?'"*

QUESTIONS

» What's one "takeaway" from this week's Landing time?

Dont let the devil rob of your past remind

» What's something you wish you understood better, and why?

The bible so when im older teach my child

» What's a failure or mistake that is still impacting your
life today?

I never listen to my brother.

» How have you seen God using a past failure or mistake to
bring something good into your life?

he made me guilty on i list

» If you were free of the things that keep you stuck, what's
something you'd start doing, and what's something you'd
stop doing?

• I'll listen to my brother
• I'll stop letting the devil come into me

NOTES AND JOURNAL SPACE

Use this space to take notes during The Landing meeting time,
or to journal your thoughts and what you've learned during
your journey through The Landing.

I'll learn to not let the devil make thing from the past in me.

the**Landing**

DENIAL
lesson two

PRINCIPLE 1:

Realize that I'm not God. I admit that I am powerless to control my tendency to do the wrong thing and that my life is unmanageable.

SCRIPTURAL TRUTHS:

"Happy are those who know they are spiritually poor"
(Matthew 5:3 GNT).

"I know that nothing good lives in me, that is, in my sinful nature. For I have the desire to do what is good, but I cannot carry it out" (Romans 7:18 NIV).

DENIAL lesson two

Throughout the Student Journal, you'll find acrostics that reflect the ideas and truths you've discussed at The Landing. One of the things we all must address on our journey is how to find freedom from our DENIAL, which hurts us in many ways:

Disables our feelings
Hiding our feelings, living in denial, freezes our emotions and binds us.

Energy lost
If you transfer the energy required to maintain your denial into learning God's truth, a healthy love for others and yourself will occur.

Negates growth
God will never waste your darkness. But he can't use it unless you step out of your denial into the light of his truth.

Isolates us from God
Our secrets and denial separate us from true fellowship with God.

Alienates us from other people
We don't reveal our true selves to others for fear of what they will think or say if they knew the real us.

Lengthens the pain
Denial allows our pain to fester and to grow and to turn into shame and guilt.

Denial is a roadblock that keeps you from discovering the freedom God wants you to experience. And God's definition of freedom may look different from the way you've thought of it before. True freedom isn't about the things you're free to do; it's about the things you're free *not* to do! You're free to *not* make the choices that mess up your life!

Truth is like surgery: It hurts but heals. God promises you in Jeremiah 30:17 (NIV): *"But I will restore you to health and heal your wounds."*

QUESTIONS

» What's one "takeaway" from this week's Landing time?

» When have you seen denial affect other people's lives? Explain.

» It's hard to see denial in your own life—when you think about it, what's the likeliest way you've struggled with denial in your life? Explain.

» Why is it so hard to let go of the coping skills you learned when you were younger?

» Who's someone who seems to have let go of their childhood coping skills—someone who seems to live free from their denial? What can you learn from them?

NOTES AND JOURNAL SPACE

Use this space to take notes during The Landing meeting time, or to journal your thoughts and what you've learned during your journey through The Landing.

the Landing

POWERLESS
lesson three

PRINCIPLE 1:
Realize that I'm not God. I admit that I am powerless to control my tendency to do the wrong thing and that my life is unmanageable.

SCRIPTURAL TRUTHS:
"Happy are those who know they are spiritually poor" *(Matthew 5:3 GNT).*

"I know that nothing good lives in me, that is, in my sinful nature. For I have the desire to do what is good, but I cannot carry it out" (Romans 7:18 NIV).

POWERLESS lesson three

Here are some decisions worth making on the journey to freedom:

Don't deny the pain. Pretending the pain isn't real won't make it go away. Removing the deep pain in your life begins by recognizing it, addressing it, and giving it to God.

Admit your powerlessness. Admitting our weaknesses is a sign of strength, a solid step forward. It's a way of agreeing with what Jesus said: *"Humanly speaking, it is impossible. But with God everything is possible" (Matthew 19:26 NLT).*

Don't play God. We create problems and get into trouble when we try to control everything in life—or when we try to control the people around us. Let God be the one in control.

Admit that you need help from others. This admission makes it easier to talk with other people, seek God's help in your life, and walk in freedom and honesty and health. Here's what David wrote in Psalm 40:12 (NIV): *"For troubles without number surround me; my sins have overtaken me, and I cannot see. They are more than the hairs of my head, and my heart fails within me."*

QUESTIONS

» What's one "takeaway" from this week's Landing time?

» When was a time you felt powerless in your life? Why?

» What did you do to make it through that time?

» Why is it sometimes so difficult for you to admit you're powerless to make the changes you really want in life?

» Why does God have more freedom to move in your life when you've admitted you're powerless?

» When have you trusted God more than yourself in a situation—what happened?

NOTES AND JOURNAL SPACE

Use this space to take notes during The Landing meeting time, or to journal your thoughts and what you've learned during your journey through The Landing.

POWERLESS

lesson four

PRINCIPLE 1:
Realize that I'm not God. I admit that I am powerless to control my tendency to do the wrong thing and that my life is unmanageable.

SCRIPTURAL TRUTHS:
"Happy are those who know they are spiritually poor"
(Matthew 5:3 GNT).

"I know that nothing good lives in me, that is, in my sinful nature. For I have the desire to do what is good, but I cannot carry it out" (Romans 7:18 NIV).

POWERLESS lesson four

When you admit that you are POWERLESS, you'll leave behind a bunch of junk that can make your life miserable:

Pride
Our false pride undermines our faith, and it cuts us off from God and others.

Only ifs
Have you ever had a case of the "only ifs" (or the "if onlys")?

Worry
All worrying is a form of not trusting God enough!

Escape
We've already tried to escape and hide from our hurts, habits, and hang-ups.

Resentment
Resentments can act like emotional cancer.

Loneliness
Do you know that loneliness is a choice?

Emptiness
When you finally admit that you are truly powerless by yourself, that empty feeling inside will begin to go away.

Selfishness
Simply said, selfishness is at the heart of most problems between people.

Separation
Some people talk about finding God—as if he could ever be lost.

Look through that list. Does it describe your life right now? If it does, that's OK—you're just starting this journey. Change doesn't happen overnight. That's tough to remember because you're part of a generation that's used to getting food right away, downloading music with a click, and connecting with friends through instant communication.

God's work takes time; The Landing is a place where you can experience God's transformation. *"The time is coming when everything that is covered up will be revealed, and all that is secret will be made known to all. Whatever you have said in the dark will be heard in the light, and what you have whispered behind closed doors will be shouted from the housetops for all to hear!" (Luke 12:2-3 NLT).*

God has the power to change your life!

QUESTIONS

» What's one "takeaway" from this week's Landing time?

» What's something that you've really wrestled with God about? Why?

» The Bible says God is always with us—so what makes you still feel so lonely at times?

» What or who typically makes you feel good about who you are? Why?

» What's risky or dangerous about trusting anything besides God to make you feel good about who you are?

NOTES AND JOURNAL SPACE

Use this space to take notes during The Landing meeting time, or to journal your thoughts and what you've learned during your journey through The Landing.

the**Landing**

HOPE
lesson five

PRINCIPLE 2:
Earnestly believe that God exists, that I matter to him, and that he has the power to help me recover.

SCRIPTURAL TRUTHS:
"Happy are those who mourn, for they shall be comforted" *(Matthew 5:4 GNT).*

"For it is God who works in you to will and to act according to his good purpose" (Philippians 2:13 NIV).

HOPE lesson five

As you travel the path to freedom, you may have days when things feel hopeless. I have some good news—God is right there to provide you with the HOPE you need each step of the way:

Higher Power
This Higher Power has a name: Jesus!

Openness to change
Hope is making yourself available to change.

Power to change
Hope draws its power from a deep trust in God.

Expect to change
With God's help, the changes you have longed for are just *steps* away.

Jesus Christ is your Higher Power. He wants a personal, growing, meaningful friendship with you. He wants to be involved in every part of your life. Nothing is too big and nothing is too small—it all matters to Jesus. Here's what he says: *"My grace is all you need. My power works best in weakness" (2 Corinthians 12:9 NLT).*

You need to be open to God's change along this journey. Adopt a healthy, God-focused attitude: "I can change because of God's work in my life. I can experience hope today because of God's promises for tomorrow!"

» What's one "takeaway" from this week's Landing time?

» Which of the words on the full-length mirror hit on a wound in your own life?

» Why is it sometimes difficult for you to believe that you're "Made by God" and "Chosen by God"?

» When have you had even a little taste of how much God loves you? How did you experience that taste?

» What words do you wish you could actually hear God say to you? Why?

NOTES AND JOURNAL SPACE

Use this space to take notes during The Landing meeting time,
or to journal your thoughts and what you've learned during
your journey through The Landing.

HOPE
lesson six

PRINCIPLE 2:
Earnestly believe that God exists, that I matter to him, and that he has the power to help me recover.

SCRIPTURAL TRUTHS:
"Happy are those who mourn, for they shall be comforted"
(Matthew 5:4 GNT).

"For it is God who works in you to will and to act according to his good purpose" (Philippians 2:13 NIV).

Remember the acrostic for the word HOPE from last week? Here it is again:

Higher Power
This Higher Power has a name: Jesus!

Openness to change
Hope is making yourself available to change.

Power to change
Hope draws its power from a deep trust in God.

Expect to change
With God's help, the changes you have longed for are just *steps* away.

We need power to take our journey of growth and transformation. We need to remember, God is the source, not us. God has the power to transform our lives, even if it seems like an impossible task. *"For I can do everything through Christ, who gives me strength" (Philippians 4:13 NLT).* If we feel discouraged, we need to remember that we just began this journey a few weeks ago. Change *can* happen. Change *will* happen.

Keep turning to God for direction and guidance and strength and transformation. *"Guide me in your truth, and teach me, my God, my Savior. I trust you all day long" (Psalm 25:5 NCV).* Find your hope in Jesus each day.

QUESTIONS

» What's one "takeaway" from this week's Landing time?

» What's one way you've really struggled to find hope in your life?

» If you already know that Jesus died to give you hope, why do think you still struggle to experience it?

» What's one way you've actually experienced the hope God has given you?

NOTES AND JOURNAL SPACE

Use this space to take notes during The Landing meeting time, or to journal your thoughts and what you've learned during your journey through The Landing.

PEACE

lesson seven

PRINCIPLE 2:
Earnestly believe that God exists, that I matter to him, and that he has the power to help me recover.

SCRIPTURAL TRUTHS:
"Happy are those who mourn, for they shall be comforted" (Matthew 5:4 GNT).

"For it is God who works in you to will and to act according to his good purpose" (Philippians 2:13 NIV).

PEACE lesson seven

Life without Jesus can get insane, and lack peace. But with Jesus, your path to freedom will be marked by greater SANITY in your life. We can find:

Strength
Relying on our own power, our own strength is what got us into trouble in the first place.

Acceptance
We stop placing all the blame on others for our past actions and hurts.

New life
The penalty for our sins was paid in full by Jesus on the cross.

Integrity
We gain integrity as we begin to follow through on our promises.

Trust
We begin to trust in our relationships with others and God.

Your Higher Power
No matter what comes your way, together you and God can handle it!

God will give you strength to overcome your hurts, hang-ups, and habits. God will give you strength to face each day with hope and purpose. God will give you strength to get back on your feet if you stumble. *"God is our refuge and strength, an ever-present help in trouble. Therefore we will not fear"* *(Psalm 46:1-2 NIV).*

Along this journey, you will experience God's acceptance, and he will give you opportunities to accept the people around you—flaws and all. Remember: We're all works in progress!

And as you make progress, you'll find what it means to live a new life in Jesus. *"Anyone who belongs to Christ has become a new person. The old life is gone; a new life has begun!" (2 Corinthians 5:17 NLT).*

QUESTIONS

» What's one "takeaway" from this week's Landing time?

» Why do you so often rely on yourself first in stressful situations, instead of seeking God for your peace?

» What are some ways God has brought you peace during stressful situations?

» What have you learned about trusting God to help you through the pressures of your life?

NOTES AND JOURNAL SPACE

Use this space to take notes during The Landing meeting time,
or to journal your thoughts and what you've learned during
your journey through The Landing.

theLanding

PEACE
lesson eight

PRINCIPLE 2:
Earnestly believe that God exists, that I matter to him, and that he has the power to help me recover.

SCRIPTURAL TRUTHS:
"Happy are those who mourn, for they shall be comforted" *(Matthew 5:4 GNT).*

"For it is God who works in you to will and to act according to his good purpose" (Philippians 2:13 NIV).

PEACE lesson eight

As we travel the path to freedom, Jesus promises to give us the SANITY, or peace, our lives have been missing. We can find:

Strength
Relying on our own power, our own strength is what got us into trouble in the first place.

Acceptance
We stop placing all the blame on others for our past actions and hurts.

New life
The penalty for our sins was paid in full by Jesus on the cross.

Integrity
We gain integrity as we begin to follow through on our promises.

Trust
We begin to trust in our relationships with others and God.

Your Higher Power
No matter what comes your way, together you and God can handle it!

Insanity kills integrity; sanity restores it. You will begin to discover that other people can trust you to follow through, keep your word, and do the right thing. As you embrace the truth of who you are and how much you need God, your integrity will grow. So will your level of trust—and trustworthiness. *"Truthful words stand the test of time, but lies are soon exposed" (Proverbs 12:19 NLT).*

It's all rooted in a life built on the truths of Jesus—your Higher Power. *"Give your entire attention to what God is doing right now, and don't get worked up about what may or may not happen tomorrow. God will help you deal with whatever hard things come up when the time comes"* (Matthew 6:34 MSG).

QUESTIONS

» What's one "takeaway" from this week's Landing time?

» What's one way you've "mourned" in life—recognized your need for God and turned to him for help?

» What's one way you're learning to accept yourself for who you are, and one way you're learning to accept others for who they are?

» In what ways are you challenged to be consistent in life—to be the same person in every situation?

» What's one way you've learned to maintain your integrity—
your consistency—in difficult situations?

NOTES AND JOURNAL SPACE

Use this space to take notes during The Landing meeting time,
or to journal your thoughts and what you've learned during
your journey through The Landing.

TURN
lesson nine

PRINCIPLE 3:
Consciously choose to commit all my life and will to Christ's care and control.

SCRIPTURAL TRUTHS:
"Happy are the meek" (Matthew 5:5 GNT).

"Therefore, I urge you, brothers, in view of God's mercy, to offer your bodies as living sacrifices, holy and pleasing to God—this is your spiritual act of worship" (Romans 12:1 NIV).

TURN lesson nine

Choosing to follow Jesus and to travel his path to freedom means choosing to TURN everything over to God. We need to:

Trust
It's your choice, not chance, that determines your destiny. Put your faith into action!

Understand
Our understanding is limited to what we know on earth. We see now; God sees forever!

Repent
Repentance is to take God's point of view on our lives instead of our own.

New life
God has declared you "not guilty," and you no longer have to live under the power of sin!

Do you have trust issues? Most people do—especially those of us with deeply painful events in our pasts. Trust is an opportunity to put your faith in God into action. Psalm 10:14 (NLT) tells us, *"The helpless put their trust in you."* Psalm 56:3-4 (NIV) says, *"When I am afraid, I will trust in you. In God, whose word I praise, in God I trust; I will not be afraid. What can mortal man do to me?"* And Proverbs 3:5-6 (NIV) tells us, *"Trust in the Lord with all your heart and lean not on your own understanding; in all your ways acknowledge him, and he will make your paths straight."*

If you find it difficult to trust God to change your life, keep his promises, and meet your needs, each morning pray the words of Psalm 13:5 (NLT)—*"I trust in your unfailing love. I will rejoice because you have rescued me."* Once you make the decision to TURN your life over to Christ, your new life will begin!

QUESTIONS

» What's one "takeaway" from this week's Landing time?

» Why is it so important to repent of the things you've done to hurt God, yourself, and others—couldn't you just determine to stop doing those things and move on? Explain.

» Why is it so hard for you to repent?

» What have been the fruits—or good results—of moving in the opposite direction of your hurts, hang-ups, and habits?

» How can you really be sure God will forgive and accept you if you repent?

NOTES AND JOURNAL SPACE

Use this space to take notes during The Landing meeting time,
or to journal your thoughts and what you've learned during
your journey through The Landing.

TURN

lesson ten

PRINCIPLE 3:
Consciously choose to commit all my life and will to Christ's care and control.

SCRIPTURAL TRUTHS:
"Happy are the meek" (Matthew 5:5 GNT).

"Therefore, I urge you, brothers, in view of God's mercy, to offer your bodies as living sacrifices, holy and pleasing to God—this is your spiritual act of worship" (Romans 12:1 NIV).

TURN lesson ten

Last week, we began looking at the acrostic for TURN:

Trust

It's your choice, not chance, that determines your destiny. Put your faith into action!

Understand

Our understanding is limited to what we know on earth. We see now; God sees forever!

Repent

Repentance is to take God's point of view on our lives instead of our own.

New life

God has declared you "not guilty," and you no longer have to live under the power of sin!

Because we are human, we will never fully understand all the mysteries of the universe or all of God's thoughts. But we begin to develop a deeper level of understanding as we place our trust in Jesus—including understanding how much we need him every moment of the day, every step of our journey to freedom! Here's what Jesus says in Matthew 13:12 (NLT): *"To those who listen to my teaching, more understanding will be given, and they will have an abundance of knowledge."*

Understanding leads to repentance—abandoning patterns of sin and pursuing a deeper friendship with God. *"Repent! Turn away from all your offenses; then sin will not be your downfall. Rid yourselves of all the offenses you have committed, and get a new heart and a new spirit" (Ezekiel 18:30-31 NIV)*. And repentance opens the door to the new life God has in store!

QUESTIONS

» What's one "takeaway" from this week's Landing time?

» What's one way you've made a choice to follow God instead of the crowd in your life?

» What do you do when you feel pressured to choose a path contrary to God's intentions for your life?

» How do you know when you've really given your whole heart to God?

» What's the best decision you ever made?

NOTES AND JOURNAL SPACE

Use this space to take notes during The Landing meeting time, or to journal your thoughts and what you've learned during your journey through The Landing.

ACTION

lesson eleven

PRINCIPLE 3:
Consciously choose to commit all my life and will to Christ's care and control.

SCRIPTURAL TRUTHS:
"Happy are the meek" (Matthew 5:5 GNT).

"Therefore, I urge you, brothers, in view of God's mercy, to offer your bodies as living sacrifices, holy and pleasing to God—this is your spiritual act of worship" (Romans 12:1 NIV).

ACTION lesson eleven

The journey toward freedom means choosing to take ACTION:

Accept
Make the decision to establish that personal relationship with Jesus that he so desires.

Commit
Accept God's power to guide your life.

Turn it over
Not just the big things, or just the little things. Everything!

It's only the beginning
The new life that begins with this decision is followed by a lifelong process of growing as a Christian.

One day at a time
It is only in the present that change and growth can occur.

Next step
The next step is to choose to follow Jesus—and keep following Jesus!

God wants to give you a new life—a life of meaning, purpose, and significance, instead of a life weighed down by hurts, hang-ups, and habits. Here's what Jesus tells us in John 10:10 (CEV): *"A thief comes only to rob, kill, and destroy. I came so that everyone would have life, and have it in its fullest."* God also wants to give you eternal life with him in heaven.

We pray that if you haven't already decided to turn your life completely over to God, that now is the time to take ACTION in doing so. Simply pray that God would make you a new person, forgive your sins, and guide you into a new life built on a friendship with Jesus. In fact, you could read this prayer:

Dear God, I have tried to do it all in my own power, and I have failed. Today I want to take action, and turn my life over to you. I ask you to be my Lord and my Savior. I ask that you help me think less about me and my will. I want to daily turn my will over to you, to daily seek your direction and wisdom for my life. Please continue to help me overcome my hurts, hang-ups, and habits, and may that victory over them help others as they see your power at work in changing my life. Help me to do your will always. In Jesus' name I pray, Amen.

QUESTIONS

» What's one "takeaway" from this week's Landing time?

» The Bible describes our conversion as being "born again" — it's a deep change that happens in us when we repent and turn our life over to God. When have you had an experience that's like that — something that made you feel changed into something new?

» What are the obstacles or distractions of following Jesus with your life?

» What is your part in the work of conversion in your life, and what is God's part?

» What is the evidence of this change in your life?

NOTES AND JOURNAL SPACE

Use this space to take notes during The Landing meeting time, or to journal your thoughts and what you've learned during your journey through The Landing.

ACTION
lesson twelve

PRINCIPLE 3:
Consciously choose to commit all my life and will to Christ's care and control.

SCRIPTURAL TRUTHS:
"Happy are the meek" (Matthew 5:5 GNT).

"Therefore, I urge you, brothers, in view of God's mercy, to offer your bodies as living sacrifices, holy and pleasing to God—this is your spiritual act of worship" (Romans 12:1 NIV).

ACTION lesson twelve

The journey toward freedom means choosing to take ACTION:

Accept
Make the decision to establish that personal relationship with Jesus that he so desires.

Commit
Accept God's power to guide your life.

Turn it over
Not just the big things, or just the little things. Everything!

It's only the beginning
The new life that begins with this decision is followed by a lifelong process of growing as a Christian.

One day at a time
It is only in the present that change and growth can occur.

Next step
The next step is to choose to follow Jesus—and keep following Jesus!

God doesn't force you to follow Jesus; he gives you the freedom to make that choice—but it's the best choice you can ever make in life! Have you decided to accept God's gift of salvation and new life through Jesus? Have you committed to following Jesus with everything you have? Have you chosen to turn over all your hurts, hang-ups, and habits to God?

Your journey with God is a lifelong adventure; this is just the beginning. Walk with God every day, find your strength in your friendship with him, and keep obeying as he leads you one step at a time. *"Teach me to do your will, for you are my God; may your good Spirit lead me on level ground"* (Psalm 143:10 NIV).

QUESTIONS

» What's one "takeaway" from this week's Landing time?

» What are some examples of things that keep people from "running the race" with God?

» Why is it so difficult for you to get rid of your sins—your destructive habits and hurtful choices—on your own?

» When have you made a decision to give up something valuable to you? Why did you make that decision?

NOTES AND JOURNAL SPACE

Use this space to take notes during The Landing meeting time, or to journal your thoughts and what you've learned during your journey through The Landing.

the Landing

HONESTY
lesson thirteen

PRINCIPLE 4:
Openly examine and confess my faults to myself, to God, and to someone I trust.

SCRIPTURAL TRUTHS:
"Happy are the pure in heart" (Matthew 5:8 GNT).

"Let us examine our ways and test them, and let us return to the Lord" (Lamentations 3:40 NIV).

HONESTY lesson thirteen

Principle 4 talks about the importance of making a MORAL, or honest, inventory. Here's an acrostic summarizing five things you do at this stage of your journey to freedom:

Make time
Set aside a day or a weekend and get alone with God!

Open
Once you have seen the truth, you need to express it.

Rely
Rely on Jesus to give you the courage and strength this principle requires.

Analyze
To do a "searching and fearless" inventory, you must analyze your past honestly.

List
Your inventory is a written list of the events of your past—both good and bad.

If you want to thoroughly examine your life, set aside plenty of time to work through your inventory. Don't rush the process.

And as you spend time doing your inventory, be open to what God wants to reveal and how God may challenge and encourage you. Ask God to help you see and assess areas of guilt, dishonesty, pain, regret, fear, and resentment. And once you see these things, honestly address them. *"I cannot keep from speaking. I must express my anguish. My bitter soul must complain" (Job 7:11 NLT).* Being open allows God to do the incredible, life-changing work he wants to do.

QUESTIONS

» What's one "takeaway" from this week's Landing time?

» What's the hardest thing you've ever had to do, honesty-wise? What happened?

» What's hard about living with secrets?

» Why is it so important to "come clean" about yourself if you hope to live the life God has dreamed for you?

» What's something you'd like to "come clean" about right now?

NOTES AND JOURNAL SPACE

Use this space to take notes during The Landing meeting time, or to journal your thoughts and what you've learned during your journey through The Landing.

the Landing

HONESTY
lesson fourteen

PRINCIPLE 4:
Openly examine and confess my faults to myself, to God, and to someone I trust.

SCRIPTURAL TRUTHS:
"Happy are the pure in heart" (Matthew 5:8 GNT).

"Let us examine our ways and test them, and let us return to the Lord" (Lamentations 3:40 NIV).

HONESTY lesson fourteen

Let's wrap up the acrostic for MORAL that we introduced last week. These are things you do when you reach this stage of your journey to freedom:

Make time
Set aside a day or a weekend and get alone with God!

Open
Once you have seen the truth, you need to express it.

Rely
Rely on Jesus to give you the courage and strength this principle requires.

Analyze
To do a "searching and fearless" inventory, you must analyze your past honestly.

List
Your inventory is a written list of the events of your past—both good and bad.

Instead of relying on your own strength to change, rely on Jesus. We know that this can be a tough idea to put into practice. But that last word is the key: practice. Each day, find a way to practice relying on Jesus. Ask for his help and strength and wisdom and direction. And at the end of the day, thank him for how he's been with you through that day.

It's also important to list and analyze where you've been and what you've done—not to get down on yourself but to honestly examine your life. And don't focus on just the negative stuff; remember the positive events and experiences, too.

QUESTIONS

» What's one "takeaway" from this week's Landing time?

» It's easy to receive mercy but really hard to offer it—what was one time you received mercy, and one time you gave it?

» How have you taken God's mercy for granted, and how have you appreciated it?

» What's something you want to be honest with God about right now?

NOTES AND JOURNAL SPACE

Use this space to take notes during The Landing meeting time, or to journal your thoughts and what you've learned during your journey through The Landing.

the Landing

COMMUNITY
lesson fifteen

PRINCIPLE 4:
Openly examine and confess my faults to myself, to God, and to someone I trust.

SCRIPTURAL TRUTHS:
"Happy are the pure in heart" (Matthew 5:8 GNT).

"Let us examine our ways and test them, and let us return to the Lord" (Lamentations 3:40 NIV).

COMMUNITY lesson fifteen

Who's walking with you?

The Bible encourages us to find companions for the journey of life who root for us and want the best for us. The journey to freedom especially requires friends who are more than just travel companions; you need friends who will participate in the adventure and help you succeed and grow.

Here's what Proverbs 27:17 (NLT) says: "As iron sharpens iron, so a friend sharpens a friend." True friends understand the value of Christ-focused accountability. They keep you honest, encourage you to consistently attend The Landing, ask Jesus-focused questions, and talk to you about the value of serving others. They help you stick to the right path—and avoid destructive, dangerous paths.

At The Landing, you'll find these kinds of friends—and as you keep traveling this road, you'll experience the rewards of their support, dedication, and commitment to following Jesus!

QUESTIONS

» What's one "takeaway" from this week's Landing time?

» What's the hardest thing about finding and keeping good friendships?

» Why are so many friendships in the Christian community so shallow?

» How have your own friendships helped you in your journey toward the life God has for you?

» How have some your friendships actually hindered you?

» Why would God create you to need the friendships of others, instead of making you self-sufficient?

NOTES AND JOURNAL SPACE

Use this space to take notes during The Landing meeting time, or to journal your thoughts and what you've learned during your journey through The Landing.

COMMUNITY

lesson sixteen

PRINCIPLE 4:
Openly examine and confess my faults to myself, to God, and to someone I trust.

SCRIPTURAL TRUTHS:
"Happy are the pure in heart" (Matthew 5:8 GNT).

"Let us examine our ways and test them, and let us return to the Lord" (Lamentations 3:40 NIV).

COMMUNITY lesson sixteen

Being part of a healthy community of Christ-followers is essential on your journey to freedom. But how do you recognize a truly *healthy* group of Christians? Here are some character qualities you'll probably observe:

» Consistency
» Personal and spiritual growth
» Concern for others
» Compassion and grace
» A heart to listen to your biggest struggles and your deepest dreams
» Willingness to confront you when necessary and to offer wisdom and advice
» Vulnerability and openness

This isn't a complete list, but if you find people who demonstrate these qualities, you've probably connected with a solid group.

"Two people are better off than one, for they can help each other succeed. If one person falls, the other can reach out and help. But someone who falls alone is in real trouble. Likewise, two people lying close together can keep each other warm. But how can one be warm alone? A person standing alone can be attacked and defeated, but two can stand back-to-back and conquer. Three are even better, for a triple-braided cord is not easily broken" (Ecclesiastes 4:9-12 NLT).

QUESTIONS

» What's one "takeaway" from this week's Landing time?

» Who's someone you know whose "walk matches his or her talk"—how do you know it does?

» What are the indicators of a growing relationship with Jesus Christ?

» When has someone helped you on your journey toward freedom and close relationship with God?

» What's the difference between compassion and pity?

» How do you know when you're talking to a good listener—what "cues" do you pick up that the person is listening well to you?

» When have you confronted a friend's or family member's issues? What happened? What is the value of confrontation in relationships?

» What does it mean, and not mean, to offer suggestions to others who are struggling to stay on the road to God's best for them?

» Why are some people able to share about their struggles, while others hide them?

NOTES AND JOURNAL SPACE

Use this space to take notes during The Landing meeting time, or to journal your thoughts and what you've learned during your journey through The Landing.

INVENTORY
lesson seventeen

PRINCIPLE 4:
Openly examine and confess my faults to myself, to God, and to someone I trust.

SCRIPTURAL TRUTHS:
"Happy are the pure in heart" (Matthew 5:8 GNT).

"Let us examine our ways and test them, and let us return to the Lord" (Lamentations 3:40 NIV).

INVENTORY lesson seventeen

As you spend time in your Personal Inventory, you may encounter moments of fear or worry—even if you've successfully battled that emotion a month, week, or day earlier. This is a recurring battle along the path to freedom because we face an enemy who wants us to get discouraged, fearful, disappointed, worried, anxious, and distracted!

Memorizing verses from the Bible is a powerful way to stay focused on difficult days. Memorize this verse as a weapon to use in those moments you feel weak and ready to quit: *"Don't be afraid, for I am with you. Don't be discouraged, for I am your God. I will strengthen you and help you. I will hold you up with my victorious right hand" (Isaiah 41:10 NLT).*

And don't forget the community of fellow travelers we've talked about in recent weeks. Turn to them for prayer, strength, encouragement, and support. That's why they're there!

QUESTIONS

» What's one "takeaway" from this week's Landing time?

NOTE: You'll actually start filling out the following pages next week at The Landing. But, go ahead and start familiarizing yourself with each column.

TAKING AN HONEST AND SPIRITUAL INVENTORY

COLUMN 1	COLUMN 2
THE PERSON	**THE CAUSE**
List the people in your life that you are angry with, that have hurt you, or that you fear. Go as far back as you can.	List the specific actions that someone did to hurt you. What did the person do to cause you resentment or fear?

COLUMN 3	COLUMN 4
THE EFFECT	THE DAMAGE
Write how specific hurtful actions affected your life both in the past and in the present.	Write what the damage looks like in three particular areas: Social, Security, and Sexual.

COLUMN 5

MY PART

What part of the anger, hurt, or pain are you responsible for?

COLUMN 6

THE GOOD STUFF

Write down the positive things that have happened to you, including healed relationships, changes you've made since coming to The Landing, and so on.

NOTES AND JOURNAL SPACE

Use this space to take notes during The Landing meeting time, or to journal your thoughts and what you've learned during your journey through The Landing.

INVENTORY

lesson eighteen

PRINCIPLE 4:
Openly examine and confess my faults to myself, to God, and to someone I trust.

SCRIPTURAL TRUTHS:
"Happy are the pure in heart" (Matthew 5:8 GNT).

"Let us examine our ways and test them, and let us return to the Lord" (Lamentations 3:40 NIV).

INVENTORY lesson eighteen

Do you celebrate perfection or progress?

Many people in our world have set an unrealistic goal of perfection—the perfect grades, the perfect body, the perfect college, and so on.

Unfortunately, we are imperfect beings. That's why we need to learn to celebrate progress. Read these words from the Apostle Paul:

"Every time I think of you, I give thanks to my God. Whenever I pray, I make my requests for all of you with joy, for you have been my partners in spreading the Good News about Christ from the time you first heard it until now. And I am certain that God, who began the good work within you, will continue his work until it is finally finished on the day when Christ Jesus returns" (Philippians 1:3-6 NLT).

If you give God the freedom, he will continue working in your life. So find a reason today to celebrate progress on your journey to freedom—no matter how big or small the progress is.

QUESTIONS

» What's one "takeaway" from this week's Landing time?

» What was hard about writing your inventory?

» What felt good about this exercise?

» What's one thing you learned about yourself in while writing your inventory?

» How did you sense God's presence and comfort during this exercise?

» What impact do you expect this exercise to have on your life?

NOTES AND JOURNAL SPACE

Use this space to take notes during The Landing meeting time, or to journal your thoughts and what you've learned during your journey through The Landing.

SPIRITUAL INVENTORY

lesson nineteen

PRINCIPLE 4:
Openly examine and confess my faults to myself, to God, and to someone I trust.

SCRIPTURAL TRUTHS:
"Happy are the pure in heart" (Matthew 5:8 GNT).

"Let us examine our ways and test them, and let us return to the Lord" (Lamentations 3:40 NIV).

SPIRITUAL INVENTORY lesson nineteen

What matters most in your life?

Maybe you've never answered that question in writing, but your daily choices reveal what matters most to you—your priorities, your values, your passions, your dreams.

What value do you place on your relationships with other people? How are you developing healthier friendships? How willingly do you forgive people who've hurt you?

What matters more: impressing other people or serving other people? As a follower of Jesus, are there still areas of life that you're holding on to, instead of fully surrendering to God? Is your attitude growing increasingly better or bitter?

If any of those questions resonate with you, spend a few minutes praying for God's help to continue growing in that area. God enjoys it when you share your deepest thoughts with him and seek his help on the path to freedom.

QUESTIONS

» What matters most in your life?

» What's one "takeaway" from this week's Landing time?

» As you've grown in your relationship to God, how have your priorities in life changed? How have they stayed the same?

» When you think of your current priorities, what do you feel good about? What do you feel bad about?

» In what circumstances is it hard for you to maintain a good attitude?

» What's one way your attitude has changed as you've grown closer to God?

NOTES AND JOURNAL SPACE

Use this space to take notes during The Landing meeting time, or to journal your thoughts and what you've learned during your journey through The Landing.

SPIRITUAL INVENTORY

lesson twenty

PRINCIPLE 4:
Openly examine and confess my faults to myself, to God, and to someone I trust.

SCRIPTURAL TRUTHS:
"Happy are the pure in heart" (Matthew 5:8 GNT).

"Let us examine our ways and test them, and let us return to the Lord" (Lamentations 3:40 NIV).

SPIRITUAL INVENTORY lesson twenty

Proverbs 10:9 (NLT) in the Bible tells us: *"People with integrity walk safely, but those who follow crooked paths will slip and fall."* Those words remind us of integrity's role in keeping ourselves focused as we walk the path to freedom.

Maybe you don't use the word "integrity" much in conversation with friends, but you understand the idea. It means being consistent, honest, reliable, and honorable. It means that the person you are on Sunday mornings or at The Landing is the same person you are on the weekends or in middle of the school day.

The battle for integrity begins in the mind. *"Dear friends, God is good. So I beg you to offer your bodies to him as a living sacrifice, pure and pleasing. That's the most sensible way to serve God. Don't be like the people of this world, but let God change the way you think. Then you will know how to do everything that is good and pleasing to him"* (Romans 12:1-2 CEV).

God will help you think differently. New thoughts will lead to new actions and choices and patterns—which will lead to a life of integrity and consistency.

QUESTIONS

» What's one "takeaway" from this week's Landing time?

» What are some things about your life that have made it hard to believe that God truly loves you?

» When you think about your life, in what ways have you sacrificed your integrity?

» How well have you guarded your mind in the past?

» As you have shifted away from the things that "muddy up" your mind and focus more on God's truths, how has your life been impacted?

NOTES AND JOURNAL SPACE

Use this space to take notes during The Landing meeting time, or to journal your thoughts and what you've learned during your journey through The Landing.

SPIRITUAL INVENTORY

lesson twenty-one

PRINCIPLE 4:
Openly examine and confess my faults to myself, to God, and to someone I trust.

SCRIPTURAL TRUTHS:
"Happy are the pure in heart" (Matthew 5:8 GNT).

"Let us examine our ways and test them, and let us return to the Lord" (Lamentations 3:40 NIV).

SPIRITUAL INVENTORY lesson twenty-one

The journey to freedom is a journey toward health and healing. It's an opportunity for God to make you whole and well in all areas of life.

Most people think about "health" as being a physical issue. They're right, of course. It's important to have a body that is healthy because of what you eat, how often you exercise, and how much you sleep each night. It's additionally important if you have a history of destructive habits.

But you also need healthy relationships with family members. This can be difficult if your family has deep secrets or dysfunctional patterns. Do your best, and ask for God's help as you seek reconciliation and forgiveness.

A healthy attitude toward your church or youth group is also valuable. *"Some people have gotten out of the habit of meeting for worship, but we must not do that. We should keep on encouraging each other, especially since you know that the day of the Lord's coming is getting closer" (Hebrews 10:25 CEV).* You can find encouragement, support, and friendship as you spend time with other Christ-followers.

QUESTIONS

» What's one "takeaway" from this week's Landing time?

» Do you have, generally speaking, a healthy or unhealthy relationship with your own body? In what ways have you mistreated your body? What activities or habits have caused harm to your physical health?

» Do you have, generally speaking, a healthy or unhealthy relationship with your family? Explain.

» What's the hardest thing about staying committed to your church or youth group?

» What are some fruits you've seen in your life because of your commitment to church?

NOTES AND JOURNAL SPACE

Use this space to take notes during The Landing meeting time, or to journal your thoughts and what you've learned during your journey through The Landing.

CELEBRATION

lesson twenty-two

CELEBRATION lesson twenty-two

JOURNAL SPACE

As you celebrated this week, what were some of your thoughts and feelings about your journey at The Landing?

theLanding

PRAYER STATIONS
lesson twenty-three

PRAYER STATIONS lesson twenty-three

Have you prayed today?

Please don't feel guilty if you haven't. But don't miss out because prayer is such a wonderful experience on the journey to freedom.

If you haven't made time to pray yet, do it right now. Tell God three reasons you're thankful. Share three areas of need in your life. Pray for God to help three specific friends. Then pause for three minutes of silence to see what God might reveal or speak to you.

And if you've already prayed, go ahead and do it again anyway—a little extra prayer on the journey to freedom is never a bad thing!

QUESTIONS

» What's one "takeaway" from this week's Landing time?

» What are some ways you can see evidence in people's lives that they're searching for God and meaning?

» What's one way you've helped someone in your life?

» In what ways is God trying to reach you right now in your life?

» Which people come to mind who seem "sent from God" to intersect your life and lead you to be more like Jesus? List them and give an example.

NOTES AND JOURNAL SPACE

Use this space to take notes during The Landing meeting time, or to journal your thoughts and what you've learned during your journey through The Landing.

the**Landing**

CONFESS
lesson twenty-four

PRINCIPLE 4:
Openly examine and confess my faults to myself, to God, and to someone I trust.

SCRIPTURAL TRUTHS:
"Happy are the pure in heart" (Matthew 5:8 GNT).

"Therefore confess your sins to each other and pray for each other so that you may be healed" (James 5:16 NIV).

CONFESS lesson twenty-four

Don't give up.

In your darkest moment, those words may be what you most need to hear. When you feel helpless and hopeless, overwhelmed and targeted, make the choice to keep going for one more day, one more hour, one more minute.

"Dear brothers and sisters, when troubles come your way, consider it an opportunity for great joy. For you know that when your faith is tested, your endurance has a chance to grow. So let it grow, for when your endurance is fully developed, you will be perfect and complete, needing nothing" (James 1:2-4 NLT).

Persevere. Endure. Stand strong. You're not alone. You can make it. Friends are there. God is there. God will give you strength.

Don't give up.

QUESTIONS

» What's one "takeaway" from this week's Landing time?

» When you think about the experiences you had at the four stations, what's one thing you confessed that was new or surprising for you?

» What are you learning from completing your Personal and Spiritual Inventory?

» Is it enough to confess your sins in private, or is it important to confess them to another person? Explain.

» How does confession make you stronger?

» How does confession make you freer?

NOTES AND JOURNAL SPACE

Use this space to take notes during The Landing meeting time, or to journal your thoughts and what you've learned during your journey through The Landing.

the**Landing**

CONFESS
lesson twenty-five

PRINCIPLE 4:
Openly examine and confess my faults to myself, to God, and to someone I trust.

SCRIPTURAL TRUTHS:
"Happy are the pure in heart" (Matthew 5:8 GNT).

"Therefore confess your sins to each other and pray for each other so that you may be healed" (James 5:16 NIV).

CONFESS lesson twenty-five

What does it take to truly CONFESS that you need help from God and from others?

Confess your shortcomings, resentments, and sins
Come clean and admit that wrong is wrong.

Obey God's direction
Confession means that we agree with God regarding our sins.

No more guilt
The verdict is in! *"All have sinned;... yet God declares us 'not guilty'... if we trust in Jesus Christ, who freely takes away our sins" (Romans 3:23-24 TLB).*

Face the truth
Confession *requires* honesty.

Ease the pain
When we share our secrets, we begin to lessen the pain and shame.

Stop the blame
Our secrets have isolated us from each other long enough!

Start accepting God's forgiveness
Once we accept God's forgiveness, we are able to look others in the eye.

Confession means recognizing and admitting past mistakes and seeking God's help as you move forward. Instead of trying to make it on your own, find support. Instead of hiding sin, expose it to God and trusted friends. *"Confess your sins to*

each other and pray for each other so that you may be healed"
(James 5:16 NIV).

Instead of seeing yourself as a failure, recognize God's love
and forgiveness and ability to make you whole and help you
live wisely. *"For the Lord grants wisdom! From his mouth
come knowledge and understanding. He grants a treasure of
common sense to the honest. He is a shield to those who walk
with integrity. He guards the paths of the just and protects
those who are faithful to him" (Proverbs 2:6-8 NLT).*

QUESTIONS

» What's one "takeaway" from this week's Landing time?

» Why is it sometimes hard to believe that your sins are truly
"washed away"?

» How would you feel if you forgave someone for something
they'd done to you, but they refused to forgive themselves?

NOTES AND JOURNAL SPACE

Use this space to take notes during The Landing meeting time, or to journal your thoughts and what you've learned during your journey through The Landing.

ADMIT
lesson twenty-six

PRINCIPLE 4:
Openly examine and confess my faults to myself, to God, and to someone I trust.

SCRIPTURAL TRUTHS:
"Happy are the pure in heart" (Matthew 5:8 GNT).

"Therefore confess your sins to each other and pray for each other so that you may be healed" (James 5:16 NIV).

ADMIT lesson twenty-six

"I'm wrong." "I messed up." "I blew it."

Those are tough phrases to say, aren't they? We all want to be right all the time. We all want to make the best decisions all the time. But it doesn't happen—especially if we're working to overcome our hurts, hang-ups, and habits.

Admitting your faults to another person is a huge step—but it's a healing step. It opens the door to deeper community and connection. It helps you pursue a life of humility and forgiveness. You begin facing your life honestly. And you discover that others have traveled the same path you're walking—or they're walking right alongside you.

It's a risky step, but it's better than the alternative—holding on to our secrets. *"When I refused to confess my sin, my body wasted away, and I groaned all day long. Day and night your hand of discipline was heavy on me. My strength evaporated like water in the summer heat" (Psalm 32:3-4 NLT).*

Refer to p. 116 of this journal to help find a safe person to listen to your Personal and Spiritual Inventory.

QUESTIONS

» What's one "takeaway" from this week's Landing time?

» Why is it "not enough" to simply determine to stop sinning in your life? Why is it so important to admit your sins to another person you trust?

» What's the hardest aspect when you think about admitting your sins to someone?

» What's the hardest aspect of admitting your wrongs and failures to someone?

NOTES AND JOURNAL SPACE

Use this space to take notes during The Landing meeting time, or to journal your thoughts and what you've learned during your journey through The Landing.

ADMIT
lesson twenty-seven

PRINCIPLE 4:
Openly examine and confess my faults to myself, to God, and to someone I trust.

SCRIPTURAL TRUTHS:
"Happy are the pure in heart" (Matthew 5:8 GNT).

"Therefore confess your sins to each other and pray for each other so that you may be healed" (James 5:16 NIV).

ADMIT lesson twenty-seven

It's time to find a trustworthy person to meet with—someone who will listen to your inventory without judging you, someone who will extend God's grace to you.

The person you choose needs to be someone of the same gender who's a Christ-follower; it also helps if this person has gone through a program like The Landing or is familiar with the kinds of truths and teachings we're experiencing.

Once you've identified the person you'd like to share your story with, talk with an accountability friend or a leader in The Landing. Ask for any feedback on the person you've chosen. Then arrange a time and place to meet with the person who will hear your story.

When you meet with this trustworthy person, take time to pray together. As you share your story and confess your inventory, also talk about how God has guided you and about positive moments along the way. Be honest as your friend asks you any follow-up questions. Make sure to pray again as you close your time together. And thank your friend for taking the time to hear your story.

QUESTIONS

» What's one "takeaway" from this week's Landing time?

» If you never admitted your own responsibility for the hurts, hang-ups, and habits in your life, how would that impact your relationships?

» Why is God so interested in dragging your sins out of the shadows and into the light?

» Forgiveness isn't always easy to accept—what makes it difficult to receive mercy from God and others?

» Is it possible to feel completely "clean" in life? Why or why not?

» When have you felt "clean" in your life, and why did you feel that way?

NOTES AND JOURNAL SPACE

Use this space to take notes during The Landing meeting time, or to journal your thoughts and what you've learned during your journey through The Landing.

READY
lesson twenty-eight

PRINCIPLE 5:
Voluntarily submit to every change God wants to make in my life and humbly ask him to remove my character defects.

SCRIPTURAL TRUTHS:
"Happy are those whose greatest desire is to do what God requires" (Matthew 5:6 GNT).

"Humble yourselves before the Lord, and he will lift you up" (James 4:10 NIV).

READY lesson twenty-eight

Here's a big question: Are you READY to let God make the changes he wants and remove the character defects that are in the way? Think about the process this way:

Release control

God won't clean up an area of your life unless you are willing to ask him in.

Easy does it

Allow God time to work in your life.

Accept the change

Seeing the need for change and allowing the change to occur are two different things.

Do replace your character defects

If you don't, you make yourself vulnerable for the return of a negative character defect.

Yield to the growth

It is the Holy Spirit's work within you.

When you started The Landing, you probably thought you enjoyed being in control. But trying to control our own lives is what got us into trouble in the first place. God asks you to release control to him in order to create the change he desires—the change you need.

"Joyful are people of integrity, who follow the instructions of the Lord. Joyful are those who obey his laws and search for him with all their hearts. They do not compromise with evil, and they walk only in his paths" (Psalm 119:1-3 NLT).

120 JOURNAL

Allow God to work in your life. You may feel like you're only taking "baby steps" on the journey to freedom, but God has a plan and purpose. The change will come! *"Commit everything you do to the Lord. Trust him, and he will help you"* (Psalm 37:5 NLT).

QUESTIONS

» What's one "takeaway" from this week's Landing time?

» Is there anything in your life you're afraid to let go of?

» What is the first change you're ready to have God help you with?

» Based on your experiences, how and why do some people experience profound change—for the better—in their lives?

NOTES AND JOURNAL SPACE

Use this space to take notes during The Landing meeting time, or to journal your thoughts and what you've learned during your journey through The Landing.

READY

lesson twenty-nine

PRINCIPLE 5:
Voluntarily submit to every change God wants to make in my life and humbly ask him to remove my character defects.

SCRIPTURAL TRUTHS:
"Happy are those whose greatest desire is to do what God requires" (Matthew 5:6 GNT).

"Humble yourselves before the Lord, and he will lift you up" (James 4:10 NIV).

READY

Last week, we began seeing what it meant to be READY for the process of change that God wants in our lives:

Release control
God won't clean up an area of your life unless you are willing to ask him in.

Easy does it
Allow God time to work in your life.

Accept the change
Seeing the need for change and allowing the change to occur are two different things.

Do replace your character defects
If you don't, you make yourself vulnerable for the return of a negative character defect.

Yield to the growth
It is the Holy Spirit's work within you.

Once you get rid of "junk" in your life, it's important to replace those defects with positive, beneficial, life-giving habits and patterns. Look for ways to serve other people. Spend time with other Christ-followers. Direct your energy toward activities that will aid you on the journey to freedom.

"God's children cannot keep on being sinful. His life-giving power lives in them and makes them his children, so that they cannot keep on sinning" (1 John 3:9 CEV).

And then get ready for what God has planned for you!

QUESTIONS

» What's one "takeaway" from this week's Landing time?

» What are some things that keep you from taking risks on in this journey toward freedom?

» Why is it relatively easy to talk about change, but hard to actually make the changes?

» What can you do today to show God that you're willing to take risks to make changes in your life?

NOTES AND JOURNAL SPACE

Use this space to take notes during The Landing meeting time,
or to journal your thoughts and what you've learned during
your journey through The Landing.

VICTORY
lesson thirty

PRINCIPLE 5:
Voluntarily submit to every change God wants to make in my life and humbly ask him to remove my character defects.

SCRIPTURAL TRUTHS:
"Happy are those whose greatest desire is to do what God requires" (Matthew 5:6 GNT).

"Humble yourselves before the Lord, and he will lift you up" (James 4:10 NIV).

"If we confess our sins, he is faithful and just and will forgive us our sins and purify us from all unrighteousness" (1 John 1:9 NIV).

VICTORY lesson thirty

We all need to take time to recognize the "wins" along our path to freedom. That's why today we're looking at an acrostic for VICTORY:

Voluntarily submit
Voluntarily submit to every change God wants you to make in your life and humbly ask him to remove your shortcomings.

Identify character defects
Determine which character defects you want to work on first.

Change your mind
Let God transform (change) you by renewing your mind.

Turn over character defects
Turn them over to God.

One day at a time
Your lifelong hurts, hang-ups, and habits need to be worked on in 24-hour increments.

Recovery is a process
Don't look for perfection; instead rejoice in steady progress.

You must choose to change
As long as you place self-reliance first, a true reliance on Jesus Christ is impossible.

Read through that list again. Notice all the action verbs? Experiencing victory happens when we do our part—God already promises to help us change and grow and overcome, but we must take steps toward him, with him, alongside him.

The "T" in the acrostic is particularly important—turn over character defects. Don't try to fix yourself; allow God to do the fixing! God is your source for VICTORY!

QUESTIONS

» What's one "takeaway" from this week's Landing time?

» What have your past attempts to overcome your character issues or hurts, hang-ups, or habits been like?

» Most of us have exhausted ourselves trying to "get better" on our own—why is that path a hopeless one for you?

» What's something you could do every day to trust in God's power to bring you victory?

» What's the most difficult thing about trusting God to give you victory over my issues, rather than trusting yourself to do it?

NOTES AND JOURNAL SPACE

Use this space to take notes during The Landing meeting time, or to journal your thoughts and what you've learned during your journey through The Landing.

VICTORY
lesson thirty-one

PRINCIPLE 5:
Voluntarily submit to every change God wants to make in my life and humbly ask him to remove my character defects.

SCRIPTURAL TRUTHS:
"Happy are those whose greatest desire is to do what God requires" (Matthew 5:6 GNT).

"Humble yourselves before the Lord, and he will lift you up" (James 4:10 NIV).

"If we confess our sins, he is faithful and just and will forgive us our sins and purify us from all unrighteousness" (1 John 1:9 NIV).

Do you remember the acrostic for VICTORY that we saw last week? Let's look at it again:

Voluntarily submit
Voluntarily submit to every change God wants you to make in your life and humbly ask him to remove your shortcomings.

Identify character defects
Determine which character defects you want to work on first.

Change your mind
Let God transform (change) you by renewing your mind.

Turn over character defects
Turn them over to God.

One day at a time
Your lifelong hurts, hang-ups, and habits need to be worked on in 24-hour increments.

Recovery is a process
Don't look for perfection; instead rejoice in steady progress.

You must choose to change
As long as you place self-reliance first, a true reliance on Jesus Christ is impossible.

What's your most recent victory on the journey to freedom? Was it something big, or something small? Was it a victory you experienced with a friend, or with a family member, or with a group of people? Or was it a victory achieved in solitude? Take a moment right now to thank God for that victory. Give

him the honor and praise for helping you achieve this victory—
and pray for God's strength in making this a victory-filled day
and week!

QUESTIONS

» What's one "takeaway" from this week's Landing time?

» Are all hard things you go through, in the end, "worth it?"
Why or why not?

» What makes them "worth it"?

» What are some of the struggles you've been through that
you'd now say were "worth it" because of what God has
done in you?

NOTES AND JOURNAL SPACE

Use this space to take notes during The Landing meeting time, or to journal your thoughts and what you've learned during your journey through The Landing.

AMENDS
lesson thirty-two

PRINCIPLE 6:
Evaluate all my relationships. Offer forgiveness to those who have hurt me and make amends for harm I've done to others, except when to do so would harm them or others.

SCRIPTURAL TRUTHS:
"Happy are the merciful" (Matthew 5:7 GNT).

"Happy are the peacemakers" (Matthew 5:9 GNT).

"Do to others as you would have them do to you"
(Luke 6:31 NIV).

AMENDS lesson thirty-two

The idea of "making amends" may seem a bit unusual to you, but it's rooted in what Jesus said in Matthew 5:23-24. When you've made poor choices and hurt other people, this is an opportunity to restore those relationships.

This might be simple to accomplish by meeting with a family member or someone who used to be a close friend. Perhaps it requires a phone call or an e-mail to someone who lives far away.

Or it may require another kind of sacrifice. If your past includes such patterns as stealing or vandalism, making amends also means restoring the physical items you stole, damaged, or destroyed.

Whatever it takes, the process of making amends is an incredible step on the journey to freedom.

QUESTIONS

» What's one "takeaway" from this week's Landing time?

» What's your idea for making amends in your life, and how will you carry it out?

» What role does making amends play in the reconciliation process?

» Why is making amends just as important for you as for the people you make the amends to?

NOTES AND JOURNAL SPACE

Use this space to take notes during The Landing meeting time, or to journal your thoughts and what you've learned during your journey through The Landing.

AMENDS
lesson thirty-three

PRINCIPLE 6:
Evaluate all my relationships. Offer forgiveness to those who have hurt me and make amends for harm I've done to others, except when to do so would harm them or others.

SCRIPTURAL TRUTHS:
"Happy are the merciful" (Matthew 5:7 GNT).

"Happy are the peacemakers" (Matthew 5:9 GNT).

"Do to others as you would have them do to you"
(Luke 6:31 NIV).

AMENDS lesson thirty-three

If you're struggling with the idea of making amends to the people you've hurt, read and memorize Philippians 4:13 (NLT): *"For I can do everything through Christ, who gives me strength."*

When you sit across the table from the person you've hurt, picture Jesus in the seat next to you. When you pick up that phone to make a call, think of Jesus standing next to you with a hand on your shoulder. When you write that letter or type that e-mail, imagine Jesus in the room with you, offering you words of encouragement and hope.

You're not alone. Jesus is right there with you.

QUESTIONS

» What's one "takeaway" from this week's Landing time?

» Are some things just to painful and destructive to forgive? Why or why not?

» What are the components of making amends—what goes into it?

140 JOURNAL

» How do you make amends to God?

NOTES AND JOURNAL SPACE

Use this space to take notes during The Landing meeting time, or to journal your thoughts and what you've learned during your journey through The Landing.

the Landing

FORGIVENESS
lesson thirty-four

PRINCIPLE 6:
Evaluate all my relationships. Offer forgiveness to those who have hurt me and make amends for harm I've done to others, except when to do so would harm them or others.

SCRIPTURAL TRUTHS:
"Happy are the merciful" (Matthew 5:7 GNT).

"Happy are the peacemakers" (Matthew 5:9 GNT).

*"Do to others as you would have them do to you"
(Luke 6:31 NIV).*

*"Therefore, if you are offering your gift at the altar and there remember that your brother has something against you, leave your gift there in front of the altar. First go and be reconciled to your brother; then come and offer your gift"
(Matthew 5:23-24 NIV).*

FORGIVENESS lesson thirty-four

We've spent the last couple of weeks talking about making amends to people we've hurt, and the topic of forgiveness goes right along with this conversation.

We all mess up and make mistakes, and those of us traveling the path to freedom have long lists of mistakes from the past! The foundational step in the process of forgiveness is to receive God's gift of forgiveness through Jesus Christ. Have you made that important decision?

But the process continues when you examine your life and see how other's poor choices and patterns have hurt you. It's essential to offer forgiveness, too. It doesn't mean that you'll become best friends with them or that you may even spend time together—but it does mean that you've done your part to seek healing and restoration from the people you've hurt.

Yes, this is a difficult step to take. But it's a life-changing step!

QUESTIONS

» What's one "takeaway" from this week's Landing time?

» What's hard about offering forgiveness when you've been hurt? What's freeing about it?

» What has another person done to you that feels or seems too big to be forgiven? Explain.

» Is forgiveness dependent on the person who's done the wrong being willing to repent first? Why or why not?

» Why is it important to forgive yourself for the wrong things you've done?

NOTES AND JOURNAL SPACE

Use this space to take notes during The Landing meeting time, or to journal your thoughts and what you've learned during your journey through The Landing.

FORGIVENESS
lesson thirty-five

PRINCIPLE 6:
Evaluate all my relationships. Offer forgiveness to those who have hurt me and make amends for harm I've done to others, except when to do so would harm them or others.

SCRIPTURAL TRUTHS:
"Happy are the merciful" (Matthew 5:7 GNT).

"Happy are the peacemakers" (Matthew 5:9 GNT).

"Do to others as you would have them do to you"
(Luke 6:31 NIV).

"Therefore, if you are offering your gift at the altar and there remember that your brother has something against you, leave your gift there in front of the altar. First go and be reconciled to your brother; then come and offer your gift"
(Matthew 5:23-24 NIV).

FORGIVENESS lesson thirty-five

How willingly do you forgive the people who've hurt you?

Depending on your life story, this can be tough. In fact, you may want to get revenge against them. Or hold on to the pain. Or stew in your bitterness.

But consider what the Apostle Paul wrote: *"Do not repay anyone evil for evil. Be careful to do what is right in the eyes of everybody. If it is possible, as far as it depends on you, live at peace with everyone"* (Romans 12:17-18 NIV). And these words: *"Get rid of all bitterness, rage and anger, brawling and slander, along with every form of malice"* (Ephesians 4:31 NIV).

Forgiving others is a huge step forward on the journey to freedom. It's also essential to forgive yourself for mistakes you've made. God loves you. Don't let the enemy beat you up with thoughts about the past. According to what Paul writes in 2 Corinthians 5:17, God says that you're now a new creation! Let those words strengthen and encourage you today!

QUESTIONS

» What's one "takeaway" from this week's Landing time?

» How would you react to being betrayed?

» When you have withheld forgiveness, for one reason or another, how did that make you feel?

» When you have forgiven someone, what led up to that decision, and what happened after you forgave?

» Have you gone back to your Inventory sheet to see who else you need to forgive?

NOTES AND JOURNAL SPACE

Use this space to take notes during The Landing meeting time, or to journal your thoughts and what you've learned during your journey through The Landing.

the Landing

CELEBRATION
lesson thirty-six

CELEBRATION lesson thirty-six

JOURNAL SPACE

As you celebrated this week, what were some of your thoughts
and feelings about your journey at The Landing?

GRACE
lesson thirty-seven

PRINCIPLE 6:
Evaluate all my relationships. Offer forgiveness to those who have hurt me and make amends for harm I've done to others, except when to do so would harm them or others.

SCRIPTURAL TRUTHS:
"Happy are the merciful" (Matthew 5:7 GNT).

"Happy are the peacemakers" (Matthew 5:9 GNT).

"Therefore, if you are offering your gift at the altar and there remember that your brother has something against you, leave your gift there in front of the altar. First go and be reconciled to your brother; then come and offer your gift" (Matthew 5:23-24 NIV).

GRACE lesson thirty-seven

One of the most amazing things about God—and that list is really long—is his GRACE:

God's gift
Grace is a gift. Grace cannot be bought. It is freely given by God.

Received by our faith
No matter how hard we may work, we cannot earn our way into heaven.

Accepted by God's love
We can forgive others because God first forgave us.

Christ paid the price
Jesus died on the cross so that all our sins, all our wrongs, are forgiven.

Everlasting gift
Once you have chosen to follow Jesus Christ as your Savior and Lord, God's gift of grace is forever.

We cannot earn God's grace. You can be the nicest, kindest, most spiritual, most generous person on the face of the planet, but you will never earn God's grace. It's something that God chooses to give, and it's something you must choose to receive.

"For it is by grace you have been saved, through faith—and this not from yourselves, it is the gift of God—not by works, so that no one can boast" (Ephesians 2:8-9 NIV).

This week, as you're traveling the path to freedom, take time to remember how amazing God's grace truly is, and allow that realization to lead you to an even deeper, more committed relationship with God.

QUESTIONS

» What's one "takeaway" from this week's Landing time?

» Why are "bad grades" so hard to accept?

» Why do so many seem to struggle with receiving grace?

» Do you grade others the same way you grade yourself? Why or why not?

» How is God's "grading system" different from your own?

NOTES AND JOURNAL SPACE

Use this space to take notes during The Landing meeting time, or to journal your thoughts and what you've learned during your journey through The Landing.

GRACE
lesson thirty-eight

PRINCIPLE 6:
Evaluate all my relationships. Offer forgiveness to those who have hurt me and make amends for harm I've done to others, except when to do so would harm them or others.

SCRIPTURAL TRUTHS:
"Happy are the merciful" (Matthew 5:7 GNT).

"Happy are the peacemakers" (Matthew 5:9).

"Therefore, if you are offering your gift at the altar and there remember that your brother has something against you, leave your gift there in front of the altar. First go and be reconciled to your brother; then come and offer your gift" (Matthew 5:23-24 NIV).

GRACE lesson thirty-eight

We always need to celebrate God's incredible GRACE:

God's gift
Grace is a gift. Grace cannot be bought. It is freely given by God.

Received by our faith
No matter how hard we may work, we cannot earn our way into heaven.

Accepted by God's love
We can forgive others because God first forgave us.

Christ paid the price
Jesus died on the cross so that all our sins, all our wrongs, are forgiven.

Everlasting gift
Once you have chosen to follow Jesus Christ as your Savior and Lord, God's gift of grace is forever.

Every time we think about God's grace in our lives, we are reminded of how God accepts us, how Jesus paid the price for our sins, and how we have been given the incredible gift of everlasting life in heaven. Those are all huge reasons to be thankful!

"But because of his great love for us, God, who is rich in mercy, made us alive with Christ even when we were dead in transgressions—it is by grace you have been saved" (Ephesians 2:4-5 NIV).

QUESTIONS

» What's one "takeaway" from this week's Landing time?

» When have you experienced grace from someone—something that made a big difference in your life?

» When have you offered grace to someone—something that made a big difference in that person's life?

» When you first "tasted" God's grace, what happened, and how does it still impact you today?

NOTES AND JOURNAL SPACE

Use this space to take notes during The Landing meeting time,
or to journal your thoughts and what you've learned during
your journey through The Landing.

the Landing

PRAYER STATIONS

lesson thirty-nine

PRAYER STATIONS lesson thirty-nine

Face-to-face communication is one of the keys to building and sustaining a healthy friendship. I doubt you and your best friend only talk on the phone or only communicate with text messages—you understand the joy of spending time together.

God wants to spend time with you, too, and unlike the people of the Old Testament, you have direct access to God through Jesus Christ. You can go right to God with your needs and concerns and praises.

Take a few minutes right now to read Psalm 139, from your Bible. It's a prayer that David wrote about God's greatness and awesomeness.

QUESTIONS

» What's one "takeaway" from this week's Landing time?

» What parts of David's prayer in Psalm 139 jump out to you? Why?

» What's something about David that you love, based on Psalm 139?

» What's something about God that you love, based on Psalm 139?

» What does it mean for God to lead you "in the everlasting way"?

» How would you translate verses 23 and 24 into your own words?

NOTES AND JOURNAL SPACE

Use this space to take notes during The Landing meeting time, or to journal your thoughts and what you've learned during your journey through The Landing.

the Landing

CROSSROADS
lesson forty

PRINCIPLE 7:
Reserve a daily time with God for self-examination, Bible reading, and prayer in order to know God and his will for my life and to gain the power to follow his will.

SCRIPTURAL TRUTHS:
"So, if you think you are standing firm, be careful that you don't fall!" (1 Corinthians 10:12 NIV).

CROSSROADS lesson forty

As you travel the journey to freedom, how do you know which way to go when you reach a crossroad—the proverbial "fork in the road?"

These are the moments when you need wisdom from God and from trusted friends. In the past, you probably encountered problems when you made decisions on your own, without counsel and input from wise, followers of Christ—and without reading the Bible and praying for God's help.

But God is ready and willing to provide the wisdom you need. *"If you need wisdom, ask our generous God, and he will give it to you. He will not rebuke you for asking. But when you ask him, be sure that your faith is in God alone. Do not waver, for a person with divided loyalty is as unsettled as a wave of the sea that is blown and tossed by the wind" (James 1:5-6 NLT).*

QUESTIONS

» What's one "takeaway" from this week's Landing time?

» What's one way you feel like you're at a crossroads in your life right now? Explain.

» What have you observed about the way most people make big decisions? What do you like and not like about that?

» Why do some people seem to change in life, while others seem stuck forever in their old patterns?

» What are the keys to sticking with a positive change in your life?

NOTES AND JOURNAL SPACE

Use this space to take notes during The Landing meeting time, or to journal your thoughts and what you've learned during your journey through The Landing.

CROSSROADS

lesson forty-one

PRINCIPLE 7:
Reserve a daily time with God for self-examination, Bible reading, and prayer in order to know God and his will for my life and to gain the power to follow his will.

SCRIPTURAL TRUTHS:
"So, if you think you are standing firm, be careful that you don't fall!" (1 Corinthians 10:12 NIV).

CROSSROADS lesson forty-one

Let's pause for a moment and examine an acrostic for the word TEN:

Take time to do a daily inventory
This answers the "what question."

Evaluate the good and the bad
This answers the "why question."

Need to admit our wrongs promptly

Each day, spend time reflecting on your interactions, your attitudes, your actions, your motives, and your use of time.

Your "daily inventory" is something you can include during your daily time of prayer, Scripture reading, and worship—your quiet time with God.

Use a journal or this Student Journal as a place to write down both the good and bad moments of each day. Celebrate the growth you see in your life, and address the troubles that arise. Instead of waiting until next week to make amends or seek forgiveness, do it today!

QUESTIONS

» What's one "takeaway" from this week's Landing time?

» In your life, what has kept you from following God?

» What have been some of your fears of following Jesus?

» How could reading your Bible and praying help keep you focused on Jesus?

» Have you found a time of day that works for you to connect with Jesus?

» What are some of the important things God has shown you during your daily inventory?

NOTES AND JOURNAL SPACE

Use this space to take notes during The Landing meeting time, or to journal your thoughts and what you've learned during your journey through The Landing.

the Landing

DAILY INVENTORY
lesson forty-two

PRINCIPLE 7:
Reserve a daily time with God for self-examination, Bible reading, and prayer in order to know God and his will for my life and to gain the power to follow his will.

SCRIPTURAL TRUTHS:
"So, if you think you are standing firm, be careful that you don't fall!" (1 Corinthians 10:12 NIV).

DAILY INVENTORY lesson forty-two

A daily inventory is a powerful way to put your faith into action. Throughout the Bible, we are reminded of the importance of obeying God—we're even told in 1 Samuel 15:22 that obedience is more important than sacrifice!

God loves our obedience because it reveals how much we truly love God. *"But don't just listen to God's word. You must do what it says. Otherwise, you are only fooling yourselves. For if you listen to the word and don't obey, it is like glancing at your face in a mirror. You see yourself, walk away, and forget what you look like. But if you look carefully into the perfect law that sets you free, and if you do what it says and don't forget what you heard, then God will bless you for doing it"* (James 1:22-25 NLT).

Don't view the daily inventory as a requirement, obligation, or burden. See it as a tool for God's ongoing process of change and growth in your life!

QUESTIONS

» What's one "takeaway" from this week's Landing time?

» Some of these questions may help you with your journaling. Today did I:
  » maintain my peace?
  » act kindly or unkindly?
  » been faithful?
  » slip into my old hurts, hang-ups, or habits?

» Why is it so important to your growth in Christ—and your ability to move through your hurts, hang-ups, and habits—to follow this practice of a "daily inventory"?

» What are some of the things that could keep you from journaling, and what are ideas for overcoming those hurdles?

» What's something that stuck out to you in your journaling experience today?

NOTES AND JOURNAL SPACE

Use this space to take notes during The Landing meeting time, or to journal your thoughts and what you've learned during your journey through The Landing.

the**Landing**

DAILY INVENTORY
lesson forty-three

PRINCIPLE 7:
Reserve a daily time with God for self-examination, Bible reading, and prayer in order to know God and his will for my life and to gain the power to follow his will.

SCRIPTURAL TRUTHS:
"So, if you think you are standing firm, be careful that you don't fall!" (1 Corinthians 10:12 NIV).

DAILY INVENTORY lesson forty-three

Have you ever gone an entire 24 hours with constant awareness of God's work in your life?

Maybe that sounds daunting and overwhelming. But God doesn't take breaks from loving and changing us. God doesn't nap from the work of making us more complete and whole. Try to live every moment of the day with an awareness of what God is doing. Celebrate God's grace and forgiveness one day at a time. If you stumble or make a mistake, reach out your hand and allow God to pick you up, dust you off, and restore you.

"The Lord is my shepherd; I have all that I need. He lets me rest in green meadows; he leads me beside peaceful streams. He renews my strength. He guides me along right paths, bringing honor to his name" (Psalm 23:1-3 NLT).

QUESTIONS

» What's one "takeaway" from this week's Landing time?

» Today, how did I use one of the tools I've learned at The Landing in making a positive choice?

» There's a strength we can find in our weakness when we're brutally honest about life—the good and the bad. How has this kind of "weakness" produced strength in your life?

» What's something you could share with your small group that you learned by looking back over your week of journaling?

NOTES AND JOURNAL SPACE

Use this space to take notes during The Landing meeting time, or to journal your thoughts and what you've learned during your journey through The Landing.

RELAPSE
lesson forty-four

PRINCIPLE 7:
Reserve a daily time with God for self-examination, Bible reading, and prayer in order to know God and his will for my life and to gain the power to follow his will.

SCRIPTURAL TRUTHS:
"Let the word of Christ dwell in you richly"
(Colossians 3:16 NIV).

RELAPSE lesson forty-four

On the path to freedom, you may stumble and fall back into old ways of thinking or acting. But here are some choices and patterns that can help you avoid a RELAPSE:

Reserve a daily quiet time
Reserve a daily time for self-examination.

Evaluate
Evaluation needs to include your physical, emotional, relational, and spiritual health.

Listen to Jesus
Listen to Jesus for wisdom and direction.

Alone and quiet time
Set a daily appointment to be alone with God.

Plug in to God's power
Connect to God's power through prayer.

Slow down
Pause long enough to hear God's answer.

Enjoy your growth
Rejoice in and celebrate the small successes along your journey.

By now, you know your areas of weakness. You know how the enemy tries to fill your mind with doubts and fears and anxiousness and temptation. You know which people, places, media, and moments make you weakest and are not "safe" for you.

Matthew 4 tells us that even Jesus was tempted, but he overcame the temptation. He fought back using Scripture and a clear understanding of his identity.

Spending time with God each day will give you extra strength to remain strong during difficult situations. You don't have to fall back into the trap of your hurts, hang-ups, and habits. *"Watch and pray so that you will not fall into temptation. The spirit is willing, but the body is weak" (Mark 14:38 NIV).*

QUESTIONS

» What's one "takeaway" from this week's Landing time?

» What typically makes you feel lonely or isolated?

» What do you typically do to cope when you feel lonely or isolated?

» How has God been a help to you, if you have allowed him, during past times of loneliness?

» Why would God allow you to feel lonely and isolated at times in your life?

» What do you need to say to God right now?

NOTES AND JOURNAL SPACE

Use this space to take notes during The Landing meeting time, or to journal your thoughts and what you've learned during your journey through The Landing.

RELAPSE
lesson forty-five

PRINCIPLE 7:
Reserve a daily time with God for self-examination, Bible reading, and prayer in order to know God and his will for my life and to gain the power to follow his will.

SCRIPTURAL TRUTHS:
"Let the word of Christ dwell in you richly"
(Colossians 3:16 NIV).

RELAPSE lesson forty-five

Being proactive about your spiritual health can help you avoid a RELAPSE of old behavior:

Reserve a daily quiet time
Reserve a daily time for self-examination.

Evaluate
Evaluation needs to include your physical, emotional, relational, and spiritual health.

Listen to Jesus
Listen to Jesus for wisdom and direction.

Alone and quiet time
Set a daily appointment to be alone with God.

Plug in to God's power
Connect to God's power through prayer.

Slow down
Pause long enough to hear God's answer.

Enjoy your growth
Rejoice in and celebrate the small successes along your journey.

QUESTIONS

» What's one "takeaway" from this week's Landing time?

» Have you found a time everyday to meet with God to do your journaling?

» What are some of your old hurts, hang-ups, and habits that were the "Old You?"

» What are positive changes you've seen since coming to The Landing?

» Have you had a relationship improve because you've made your amends?

NOTES AND JOURNAL SPACE

Use this space to take notes during The Landing meeting time, or to journal your thoughts and what you've learned during your journey through The Landing.

the**Landing**

GRATITUDE
lesson forty-six

PRINCIPLE 7:
Reserve a daily time with God for self-examination, Bible reading, and prayer in order to know God and his will for my life and to gain the power to follow his will.

SCRIPTURAL TRUTHS:
"Let the word of Christ dwell in you richly"
(Colossians 3:16 NIV).

GRATITUDE lesson forty-six

The word "meditate" causes a variety of reactions among people, but it's a solid biblical idea that will help you on the path to freedom. What does it mean to meditate on a verse from the Bible or a character quality of God?

Ponder. Contemplate. Reflect. Consider. Ruminate. Think. Chew over. Examine. In other words, meditation is a tool for going deeper—looking for God's truth and seeing how you can apply that truth to your life.

Let's practice this. Read Psalm 62:5-8 (NLT): *"Let all that I am wait quietly before God, for my hope is in him. He alone is my rock and my salvation, my fortress where I will not be shaken. My victory and honor come from God alone. He is my refuge, a rock where no enemy can reach me. O my people, trust in him at all times. Pour out your heart to him, for God is our refuge."*

Now, consider these questions: What images fill your mind as you read this? What emotions do you experience? What does this reveal about God? What does this reveal about who you are? What do these verses tell you about your relationship with God? How can you think about these words all day? How can you apply these truths to your life? That's what meditation is all about!

QUESTIONS

» What's one "takeaway" from this week's Landing time?

» How did the leader's testimony affect you?

» What's one situation in your life that you still have a hard time finding a reason to be grateful? Explain.

» Are you generally a grateful person, or is thankfulness more of a struggle for you? Explain.

» What are some victories you can share with others?

» What have you noticed about yourself when you're living with a grateful heart, and when you're not?

NOTES AND JOURNAL SPACE

Use this space to take notes during The Landing meeting time, or to journal your thoughts and what you've learned during your journey through The Landing.

GRATITUDE

lesson forty-seven

PRINCIPLE 7:

Reserve a daily time with God for self-examination, Bible reading, and prayer in order to know God and his will for my life and to gain the power to follow his will.

SCRIPTURAL TRUTHS:

"Let the word of Christ dwell in you richly"
(Colossians 3:16 NIV).

GRATITUDE lesson forty-seven

Imagine what the world might be like if everybody lived every day as if it were Thanksgiving Day. From God's perspective, that's what we all should be trying to do! *"Be thankful in all circumstances, for this is God's will for you who belong to Christ Jesus" (1 Thessalonians 5:18 NLT).*

You've probably sat around the dinner table—or the youth group room—and talked about the reasons you're thankful on Thanksgiving. What if you made that a monthly activity—or a weekly or daily event?

Take a moment right now and think of five reasons you're thankful and express your thanks to God. If any of those reasons involve specific people, send a text message (or e-mail) and tell them why you're thankful. Get in the habit of being thankful every day!

QUESTIONS

» What's one "takeaway" from this week's Landing time?

» Why is it so easy to forget about the things that make you grateful to God?

» What's something or someone you wrote on your Gratitude List that you have a renewed thankfulness for? Explain.

» What's something you're grateful for in the midst of hardship?

NOTES AND JOURNAL SPACE

Use this space to take notes during The Landing meeting time, or to journal your thoughts and what you've learned during your journey through The Landing.

GRATITUDE LIST

Take some time to write down why you're thankful. You don't need to do this all in one sitting. As you think about additional reasons you're thankful, come back to this page and write them down.

the Landing

GIVE
lesson forty-eight

PRINCIPLE 8:
Yield myself to God to be used to bring this Good News to others, both by my example and by my words.

SCRIPTURAL TRUTHS:
"Happy are those who are persecuted because they do what God requires" (Matthew 5:10 GNT).

"Brothers, if someone is caught in a sin, you who are spiritual should restore him gently. But watch yourself, or you also might be tempted" (Galatians 6:1 NIV).

GIVE lesson forty-eight

Has your attitude been changing as you've traveled the path to freedom? Are you ready to start having an attitude of giving and serving and to begin thinking about the needs of others? Jesus set the standard. We have the privilege of following his example.

The more you give to others, the less selfish you become. The more you give to God, the more you remember how he's the source of everything and how he meets all your needs. The more you give your time, the more you appreciate the time you've been given on this earth.

"But just as you excel in everything—in faith, in speech, in knowledge, in complete earnestness and in your love for us—see that you also excel in this grace of giving" (2 Corinthians 8:7 NIV).

QUESTIONS

» What's one "takeaway" from this week's Landing time?

» What's the relationship between believing and doing?

» How is sharing your story with others a form of serving?

» How do you know who, what, when, and where God wants you to serve?

» What's one way to serve that seems "natural" for you? Explain.

NOTES AND JOURNAL SPACE

Use this space to take notes during The Landing meeting time, or to journal your thoughts and what you've learned during your journey through The Landing.

GIVE

lesson forty-nine

PRINCIPLE 8:
Yield myself to God to be used to bring this Good News to others, both by my example and by my words.

SCRIPTURAL TRUTHS:
"Happy are those who are persecuted because they do what God requires" (Matthew 5:10 GNT).

"Brothers, if someone is caught in a sin, you who are spiritual should restore him gently. But watch yourself, or you also might be tempted" (Galatians 6:1 NIV).

GIVE lesson forty-nine

If you've struggled with hurts, hang-ups, and habits, you may be thinking that you've wasted parts of your past. The good news is that by being ready to share your story, God can use those experiences for good. God is able to take our mistakes and transform them into miraculous moments in our lives and in the lives of people we meet in the years ahead! How awesome is that?

QUESTIONS

» What's one "takeaway" from this week's Landing time?

» How do you know what God wants you to give to others?

» Think of a time you took a risk by giving to someone and it paid off, and a time when it didn't work out so well. What was different between the two situations?

» How have others "fed" you in your life by giving what they had to give?

» What do you think you can learn from someone sharing their story with you?

» Are you ready to share your story? Why or why not?

NOTES AND JOURNAL SPACE

Use this space to take notes during The Landing meeting time, or to journal your thoughts and what you've learned during your journey through The Landing.

the

the Landing

YES
lesson fifty

PRINCIPLE 8:
Yield myself to God to be used to bring this Good News to others, both by my example and by my words.

SCRIPTURAL TRUTHS:
"Happy are those who are persecuted because they do what God requires" (Matthew 5:10 GNT).

"Brothers, if someone is caught in a sin, you who are spiritual should restore him gently. But watch yourself, or you also might be tempted" (Galatians 6:1 NIV).

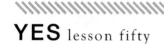

YES lesson fifty

Do you want to experience an incredible life? Get in the habit of saying YES to God:

Yield myself to God

We must give him the latitude he needs to use us as he sees fit.

Example is what is important

If you want someone to see what Christ will do for them, let them see what Christ has done for you.

Serve others as Jesus Christ did

Make your life a mission, not an intermission!

Choosing to yield to God means giving God control. It means surrendering your thoughts, motives, and actions to God.

The closer you get to God and the longer you follow Jesus, the easier it becomes to yield to God. You discover how he loves you, meets your needs, and guides your life. Instead of frustration over what God wants you to give up, you experience joy knowing that he has incredible things ahead.

"'For I know the plans I have for you,' declares the Lord, 'plans to prosper you and not to harm you, plans to give you hope and a future'" (Jeremiah 29:11 NIV).

QUESTIONS

» What's one "takeaway" from this week's Landing time?

» What's challenging about sharing your story with other people?

» How can you be encouraged by sharing your story with other people?

» What's it like to stand up—and stand out—for your faith?

» What are some ways you're already saying "YES!" to God in your life?

» What's one way others say "YES!" to God that you really admire? Explain.

NOTES AND JOURNAL SPACE

Use this space to take notes during The Landing meeting time, or to journal your thoughts and what you've learned during your journey through The Landing.

the Landing

YES
lesson fifty-one

PRINCIPLE 8:
Yield myself to God to be used to bring this Good News to others, both by my example and by my words.

SCRIPTURAL TRUTHS:
"Happy are those who are persecuted because they do what God requires" (Matthew 5:10 GNT).

"Brothers, if someone is caught in a sin, you who are spiritual should restore him gently. But watch yourself, or you also might be tempted" (Galatians 6:1 NIV).

YES lesson fifty-one

Have you spent time in the last week saying YES to God?

Yield myself to God
We must give him the latitude he needs to use us as he sees fit.

Example is what is important
If you want someone to see what Christ will do for them, let them see what Christ has done for you.

Serve others as Jesus Christ did
Make your life a mission, not an intermission!

People from your past are watching you because they've heard that you've made big changes in your life, and they're curious to see if the changes are true. People from your present are eager to see consistency between your words and actions—your faith put into practice.

If that makes you feel anxious, remember that God is the one doing the work in your life, God is the one providing you with strength each day, and God is the one who controls it all. Live your life in a way that honors God, and the rest will fall into place.

QUESTIONS

» What's one "takeaway" from this week's Landing time?

» Why is it often a surprise that God wants to move through you to impact others?

» When have you, almost accidentally, made an impact in someone's life?

» How has God encouraged you in the past, and how is he encouraging you today?

NOTES AND JOURNAL SPACE

Use this space to take notes during The Landing meeting time, or to journal your thoughts and what you've learned during your journey through The Landing.

CELEBRATION

lesson fifty-two

PRINCIPLE 8:
Yield myself to God to be used to bring this Good News to others, both by my example and by my words.

SCRIPTURAL TRUTHS:
"Happy are those who are persecuted because they do what God requires" (Matthew 5:10 GNT).

"Brothers, if someone is caught in a sin, you who are spiritual should restore him gently. But watch yourself, or you also might be tempted" (Galatians 6:1 NIV).

CELEBRATION lesson fifty-two

JOURNAL SPACE

As you celebrated this week, what were some of your thoughts and feelings about your journey at The Landing?

Use this to journal your thoughts and what you've learned during your journey through The Landing.

JOURNAL SPACE

Use this to journal your thoughts and what you've learned during your journey through The Landing.

JOURNAL SPACE

Use this to journal your thoughts and what you've learned
during your journey through The Landing.

JOURNAL SPACE

Use this to journal your thoughts and what you've learned during your journey through The Landing.

JOURNAL SPACE

Use this to journal your thoughts and what you've learned
during your journey through The Landing.

JOURNAL SPACE

Use this to journal your thoughts and what you've learned during your journey through The Landing.

Use this to journal your thoughts and what you've learned during your journey through The Landing.

JOURNAL SPACE

Use this to journal your thoughts and what you've learned
during your journey through The Landing.

Use this to journal your thoughts and what you've learned during your journey through The Landing.

JOURNAL SPACE

Use this to journal your thoughts and what you've learned during your journey through The Landing.

Use this to journal your thoughts and what you've learned during your journey through The Landing.

JOURNAL SPACE

Use this to journal your thoughts and what you've learned during your journey through The Landing.

JOURNAL SPACE

Use this to journal your thoughts and what you've learned during your journey through The Landing.

JOURNAL SPACE

Use this to journal your thoughts and what you've learned during your journey through The Landing.

JOURNAL SPACE

Use this to journal your thoughts and what you've learned during your journey through The Landing.

HELLO! ヾ(°∀°)ﾉ

JOURNAL SPACE

Use this to journal your thoughts and what you've learned during your journey through The Landing.

JOURNAL SPACE

Use this to journal your thoughts and what you've learned during your journey through The Landing.

Use this to journal your thoughts and what you've learned during your journey through The Landing.

JOURNAL SPACE

Use this to journal your thoughts and what you've learned during your journey through The Landing.

JOURNAL SPACE

Use this to journal your thoughts and what you've learned during your journey through The Landing.

JOURNAL SPA

Use this to journal your thoughts and what you've learned during your journey through The Landing.

Use this to journal your thoughts and what you've learned
during your journey through The Landing.

Salmon

Oriental Dressing

Tomatoes

Mushroom

Fried Rice

Portuguese Sausage

Carrots

green onions

eggs

Dad

7 luau leaves 1L/15

1 cs. m.d. soda

1lb. oka

Swai 3lb

veggies